THE FIRE LESSONS

THE FIRE LESSONS

Stone Flower Press, Ottawa
Cover photo: Tom Henighan
Production design: Jen Hamilton
Printed by: CreateSpace

Library and Archives Canada Cataloguing in Publication

Henighan, Tom, author
    The fire lessons / Tom Henighan.

Poems.
ISBN 978-0-9919073-4-2 (paperback)

    I. Title.

PS8565.E582F57 2016   C811'.54   C2016-901163-1

For my friends and relations, especially Marilyn, Phoebe, Steve, Lorena, Mike and Ju-Ju.

TABLE OF CONTENTS

III THE FIRE LESSONS

Epigraph

Ambition, my queer inelegant bird,
fluttering upward toward the tree-perched moon,
a cross between a buzzard and a loon,
your homing inhibitions finally lost
like feathers in a contrary wind.
Absurd, pied, sinned against and having sinned—
do you now leap toward the alluring light
to break your craven neck in a final flight?
Mad bird, launched skyward by mere rage
you would have lived far longer in your cage.

I CROSSROADS

A JOURNEY

A small boy
in the car at night
watches only the sky,
his heart beating fast
as if expecting
those pinpointing stars,
that endless black space,
to reveal some clear message
not explained by his parents.

The highway leads nowhere but home,
the car engine drones.
His heart moves
somewhere out of mind
into sadness, and no one explains.

OLD STREET IN TA'IZ

Five boys, a turbaned man,
meet a stranger with camera
in a gray Ta'iz street.
They hold up a pole made of wood—
part of a house or a cart,
a well or a plow.
They stop for a moment,
greet me with quiet looks,
their bare feet pressed tight
on the harsh stony ground.
Behind them a door no one opens
shuts out the past and the future.
One withered youth, four strong boys,
a pole man, and me,
with no chance to reclaim,
through the decades,
lost faces and bodies, buried
in war, endless murders.
A few piles of stone in the mind,
a street long forgotten.

ADVERTISEMENT FROM A MAIL ORDER CATALOG: "THE MILITARY PILOT'S WRISTWATCH"

You will like this catalog special,
a wristwatch exactly like those worn
by military pilots.
With a Swiss Ronda quartz movement,
it keeps accurate time
and sports an internal bezel
that acts as a slide rule
for advanced flight calculations.
The case is made of high grade
stainless steel, water-resistant
to ten atmospheres of pressure.
It measures air speed,
& fuel consumption,
converting nautical
or statue miles
at the pleasure
of the satisfied buyer.

With a watch like this
every flight will mean victory.
You'll cruise past civil targets,
to snuff out rockets sent your way
by angry partisans whose children
you've recently murdered.

Yet despite your toy's special features
nothing is guaranteed

to affirm love of country,
scour bloodstained streets,
or convert people due to be silenced
by your shrewd, measured fire.

And unless quite soon
the watchmaker's boasts of precision
convince you that time
is the most baleful essence of all,
your plane may still thunder on,
taking you God knows where
in the microchip world of the soul.

BACKROAD MORNING

Big-rumped and easy-eyed
the cows are half driven
in the lemon light
to fresh grass.
The rest is amble
& swinging tail.
the farmhand urges
not too ungently
the better nature
of each milk bellows
along the same rut.
Only the real workers
up at the moment
enjoy the compulsive poetry
of routine,
following back roads
to factories and stores
& shabby stations
selling gas and groceries
to common travellers.
At such an hour
of dust and shining grass
faces disappear
in the wink of a windshield
like bright thoughts
that solve no problems
but reflect the end
of a personal darkness.

THE GHOST OF PABLO NERUDA VISITS THE TAR SANDS
"DEL SUELO QUE OSCURECEN LAS PIEDRAS"
(THE WASTE THAT HIDES THE STONES)—NERUDA

Wilderness of clamps
and toothed girders exploding
the monstrous erections
on the frontiers of ice.
A skull shines like a beacon
while a nervous apprentice
unzipping his flesh,
learns quickly to plead with
the derelict paymasters.
Rubble swallows the plinth
in our eyesockets pronto,
but my spirit comes flying
at no one's command—
the stars wear out mirrors,
domed to a single breast,
the cupola shines on its amazon axis
cattle toss light on their new neon horns.
While deep in the blackening tunnels
of gimcrack the earth rolls
free from choked wells of emotion
to activate one futile sigh.
I tell you, poor hands of this empire,
stand over your anger!
Pushing wheelchairs all night
into negligent hangars,
there's no room for blind men and druggies

or any who'd pay the dire price
to unsee forever
carnivores, pageants, fouled waters.
And I trample to scorn
all uneasy rodeos
where capital horses around
with the souls of men,
where light shudders down
from a sanctified source,
the cuneiform shout
of technology's clay
adding up to the skeletal pleasure of non-existence.
Thanking God for my own
I refuse to appear
Though the feeder ramps clamor,
I refuse all diversion
such as séance
or assassination
or a basketball game.
Fleshed out beyond dreams
of the geldings of pleasure
Far from insolent innings
I refuse to appear
to the stock swingers
on their drums of symmetrical legs,
I refuse to appear
to the police in their racks of disguises
to the garrisoned mouths of politicos
brawling again in the silence
of starved lips,

I REFUSE TO APPEAR
as the ghost of a cloud,
I inhabit your sentence
I gather the seasons
I issue no rainchecks.
I refuse to appear
on the day you try out
the world's largest
sprinkler system, pardners!

AT THE NURSERY

The trees bear a part
of the silence,
fine rain drizzles down.
We plant footprints,
plod with caked shoes,
search for the perfect tree
while those fetched here
their young trunks in trim shine
beguile us, oaks and weeping birches
crab apples, spruce, maple and mulberry...
Landscapes of mind blossom earthwise,
spring billets of forest and jungle,
birds, branches, bright raindrops,
as we enter the heart of the city
all reborn like frail wood or wish—
planting, setting, sowing—
for life's unknown harvests
in the jardin des plantes
of our lost concrete world.

THE BELLS OF MALTA

In this country
twice-shaken
by history

lost faces stare
from the brazen waves.

bells ring and clang
across shining roofs

prayers weather
dust
sunlight
time.

TUBMAN'S FARM

Lennis shows me the wolf,
wild juices of words on his chin.
Though the story is simple
the mountain is big,
the maples on top
thick-leaved in season.
As down by the lake,
by the barn door—
a poor man, a novice,
in a weathered house
rambles without moving,
multiplies green.
For thirty-five years
setting traps, his boots
on the yellow floor,
the sunset woman at the stove
where he suddenly gobs.
Between ragged paws
the legend this time
at the first shot staggers.
"It's not bears I mind now,
but them wolves,
They'll take the lambs when they can get 'em."
Up the valley, out of season
winter opens wide—
Lennis shows me the wolf
gray as I expected.

THE QUIET MAN

Old Syd, old Robbie,
just coming down our street,
stopping to ponder this and that
with the mildest bald-eagle look
of amazement
at the world he's landed in.
With a short laugh in his throat
talking to Rusty the poodle
like a friendly giant,
caring about the kids,
caring about the neighbourhood.

Where did he come from?
Surely not from the square white house
plainly visible from our tiny backyard?
He must have dropped in from a village
somewhere in the Cotswolds, the Pennines,
wandered out of a slow poem
by Wordsworth, or else drifted over
from Maine, in his L.L. Bean outfit,
whose virtues he speaks of very softly
like a man who loves quality in things
untouched by any blatant praise.

Perhaps, farther back, it was different,
troopships or desert, the long war,
cruel blood-for-blood times,
separation and fear, and the first pain

of a death he would suffer much later
in a simple white house in the sunlight.
(How many up and down our street
begin to notice that he isn't here?)

Syd, there was an anger in you.
Perhaps you camped out too long
at that government desk,
denouncing the drab, the most imprecise,
language of bureaucrats:
for which they did not thank you.
Escaped from that, you found your freedom,
between the homely houses
by sure instinct driven,
feet on the right path
learning to be a presence,
taking shape as few of us can.
In the sunshine—how we miss
your ambling arrival on our doorsteps,
where we sit like shadows waiting.

You went away far too quickly.
If you should stop by once again
to chat, we're still happy to talk
about the weather,
to stand with respectful attention
while you wander away at your own speed
between the driveways and the small trees.
Adjusting your hat, hailing Rusty,
you discover a new trail, invisible to most.

Old Avondale spreads out before you
(This world's not so bad as it seems).
You stand for a minute at the corner
and just disappear.

LUMINA I

spring morning,
the sudden chill
of a hidden winter.
            *
Alive in green patches
the rotting log crumbles
at my touch.
            *
The subway's
restless limbo
of silent strangers
            *
Ghosts of wind
rock the chair
on the empty terrace
            *
My kayak bound
for an unknown lake
in the sky.
            *
A child's weathered shoe
near the crash site
nobody visits.
            *
Night at the cottage,
sounds from the deep woods
unhinge my sleep.
            *

snow in April,
two hours later, mud.
*

word poetry,
rag bags of ego
lost feelings.

THREE-PART INVENTION (GLENN GOULD AT THE PIANO)

I stagger out of bed, bedazzled,
and grope for a CD.
Figures of sound
track the beat of my body.
I dance unrepentant,
your touch forbids words.

Why should we speak in this unchanging
moment, unique and never bettered,
Bach's counterpoint beween us
and your beauty?

Here is sunlight, early autumn.
You lie naked, smiling,
the invisible master
whose hands are in motion
hums to himself
in his own remote sphere:
Inventions and *preludes*, *partitas* and *gigues*
fill the room.

Our joy lifts and then dwindles,
our artifacts useless
we grope for connections,
and suddenly earthbound, uncertain,
we talk about trivia, argue.

The pianist continues, still humming.
He is in heaven, beyond us.

At last with a smile you remind me,
"Truth lifted clean from the page.
Time made miraculous."

Then everything changes,
we wait for that climax—
strict values served by wanton art—
when lacking the distraction of each other,
we'll meet once again in this music.

WINTER

Crows call at the edges of morning.
We know what awaits them with the coming of winter:
bare stones and ice and dry bitter branches,
streets without people, the cold moon a witness
to their huddled sorrow.

Such things await us too
as we lie in the arms of a new day—
hunger and stark touch,
the death of mere comfort,
love vanquished in dreams, in tired memories.

Life's singular outpost, the mind
shows us too much or too little,
a bleak world whose light
smothers senses.
We see ourselves fall, in slow motion,
but refuse to wake up.

Crows descend to the street,
squirrels swing branches,
dogs led by dutiful neighbours
meet at the crossroads, in bare fields,
while headlines from Asia distract us,
fear rising, stocks falling,
tech warnings engulf us.

Soon we will pay to ignore them.
Trucks unload debt at the next house,
all beggars will cease to exist.
Predictions and visions cast off,
the city dissolves in its shadows.

Don't call for Jesus when the moon falls.
Accept time's betrayal, face your winter,
a blind eye fixed on the future.
The weather next week is uncertain.

MY HOSPICE

(with thanks to three women)

At this age life's worth less than joy.
Or so I thought, cruising the basement dark,
cheered that our cottage was closed now
before the new winter, our home backyard trees
still green and lovely. I hurried to put on a new disk
upstairs to let the sub-woofer blare music,
to lie down with a beer and roam through old photos,
at near eighty still dazzled by shots of my wife,
among others, with such startling white skin
that it still stops me cold. I mused those short minutes.
not remembering the sunlight, the Japanese hedge at
    the cottage,
the shining lake, the CD in my hand, my glasses in my pocket,
the rough crude floor of the basement, passed often,
and joked about. Who dumps old prints by the furnace?
When's the heavy garbage pickup, the next wash?
Then I slipped, hit the floor, and knew nothing.

I got up and fell down. Went down and looked up,
disremembered my safety, I stared at the
ceiling, my soul came up empty, as in the driveway
silence in my first fall, months before—
when I writhed at the bottom of a well, saw
sunshine, a threshold of grass to be born from.
The hospital cured me. But this time?
Stand straight though you stagger
get back to the kitchen. Find your wife, gifted dreamer,

who loves you. That's all I could think with
my monitor broken, the blood flowed.
You're in bed with a penis of rubber, nurses
decline to engage you, so you cling to the sight
of three women whose patience is endless,
who expected your death, now surprised that you shout
at them daily, while others invest you with value
you find none in the world. My wife and two friends—
soon you'll speak to all three and remember.
They imagine your needs, give full pardon
for your own silly takes on your dull life.
You must woo them intensely, asking
for nothing, showing only your faith
in their goodness, their pleasure, their sorrow.
Three ladies of virtue, unbound from compulsions
for your sake. They believe things get better,
with patience, attention, and hard work,
In their kitchens, their backyards,
half-ignored by their husbands, unrewarded,
the love they deserve maybe stuck in an old shoe.
I'll recover their virtues since with half-brain I lived
in their patience and brilliance.
I'll see their lives brighten,
as they see themselves lifted from hard times,
from tending the men who must stumble,
to the circle of goddesses, Isis and Ishtar,
Rhiannon, just neighbourhood women
who make breakfast, go shopping and keep watch,
who live on the rare shores where things gifted once
from the heart speak forever.

PRAIRIE STOP

Day explodes
in the veins of midsummer

the first and last thing's
a water tank
grafted on sky

in between coke
and gas, the attendant's
suspicious eye
a faint smell
of burning rubber

such fierce love
it is almost
hatred
dazzled in chrome
possession.

yokels in old
Chevies hauling
their weekly beans
slouch up
in awed derision

a last black splate
gunned juices &
they're off.

We follow the old
concessions
trailing their dust,
routed west
by hungers exchanged

.

YOU THERE

Picking berries in the Okanagan.
Cow-eyed Indians at home in huts
watch your thighs flake brown,
the pain of insecticide, your eye
swelling like a fat moon.
You drunk, sick. Ripped jeans,
flags of earth-heaved vines
bending stain your fingers.
Sunlight tears your hair.

In the dew-sodden morning
sweeping the huts with a stiff broom.
Radha, Radha, country girl,
the time you grow is complete
as a gourd ripening forever
to some perfection.

THE OPEONGO LINE

With thanks to Joan Finnigan

Opeongo, not a line but a dream.
The settlers came in rough ships
without consolation or comfort.
They'd been promised some land and a future.
The lumbermen watched them, shook their heads
took their contracted keep and departed.
The owners got rich and built mansions, in Ottawa,
Renfrew, beside the lakes, or on some ancient trail.
Barges swelled the river, heavy with cut wood
red pine for profit, carried away to the south,
cabins thrown up with faint hope, the shelters
on the thin barren soil left to rot when the plans failed,
a detail ignored by promoters who prophesied miracles—
it read like a swindle, as time lumbered on.

*In 1819, one Dr. Bixby arrived from Portsmouth to provide some
medical aid, and report on geology. He travelled the new land
like a gentleman, stopping with those in power, dealing with
soldiers and immigrants, eating at formal dinner parties. On a
trip through unsettled land near the Long Sault rapids Bixby
was carried by fifteen voyageurs in a 36 foot- long canoe. When
it was being portaged through the swamps, he and another
passenger decided to take a short cut through the deep woods.
They got lost and came upon an isolated cabin. The door was
opened by "a tall beautiful young woman with auburn tresses,
tidily dressed," but she spoke neither English nor French, only
Gaelic. Her brother explained that they were settlers from the*

*Scottish Highlands, the hills of Blair Athol. They missed their
homeland; the beautiful girl was sad and lonely. Bixby left.*

Poles and Scots, Germans and Irish, a few natives,
settled the valley, bears prowled at the windows of the first
huts, deer in the forest for food, wolves always hidden
but frightening, even to strong men whose crude senses
relished the fierce jokes and who went on cutting and burning,
praying and drinking. Mid-nineteenth century, the lumbermen
not always happy, as the pioneers arrive, with the govern-
ment's blessing, clear trees. The new settlers' sorrows caught
on, they were sousled by slogans, the priests drove their wag-
ons of faith, chanted the crude songs of prayer, winter snow
shut off contact with mythical cities.

*The Laird McNab arrived in the 1820s, bringing with him his
"slaves"—indentured servants—whom he shared at low wages
with his friend, Alexander MacDonnell. McNab was a scoun-
drel, exposed. But meanwhile the new settlers went about
stocking up from necessity: flour, pork, potatoes, tea and her-
rings, seed for planting. They built and kept houses, used axe
and grindstone, shovel, hoe, scythe, hand-saw and auger, and
loaded tin vessels and tin dishes, the kettles and frying pans
needed in their kitchens; blankets, sheets and quilts to keep
them warm. A wild and free-ranging crew. They danced and
played fiddles, drank and made jokes, moved on to find better
land, shook hands on their deals. Names flow out of the lost
streams: Mag Foley, the joker ("as for church, I goes when
I feels like it, Father.") Mickey Mahon, lying drunk, sipping
slowly, from a street-soiled bag of whiskey. Hank Legris and*

The big river stretching up from the capital,
plans and discussions in Parliament.
The great lake miles to the west, never reached.
The road is paved now and stretches
away through the wild. Once rough
and violent it was harried by hopefuls
but remained a wild track of ambition,

sustained by the greed of the owners,
the government cliques without conscience.

Men drank, wounded housewives, who found themselves
ugly, scratched their faces from photos, to endure as white
smears among the brave, fat smiles of the men.
The poor Irish kept drinking, matched muscles,
hatched babies with nothing to give them in the long run.
Poles, Scots, and Germans would join them.
Some died, others moved when they grew up.
They'd endured Opeongo, a mind-shaking
Canada boot-camp, where settlers touched life
with some joy, but small comfort, and built their own futures
on thin soil and wild woods. Mere power was cherished,
dreams giving way to bleak memories.

Soon the people had vanished. Nature, long-challenged,
returned. The shacks fell to earth, the trails disappeared in
the bush. A high soaring hawk over Hurd's Lake, a loon's
cry. Shallow shore water, ponds and dead trees. Animals and
plants join the cycles, die, decomposing. Dead cedars tipped
into water, light on the iron-gray cedar branches, splotches of
green moss on the topsides of branches, grassy tufts under-
water, float to the surface.

*We visit the Tubmans, old friends. Padlock on gate, mailbox
gone. House gone, a burned-out ruin. Barbed wire fence around
the garden, but plants still in bloom. We walk to the waterfall,
rushing and sudsy, it still flows, flows better than ever, A toad
sits there, gaping. The lake is hardly visible, so overgrown,*

*heavy. The maple grove stands on the hill. Most of the buildings
are wrecked now. We found the old couple, Emma and Lennis,
in a nearby village. "They'd be happy with a tarpaper shack,"
a half-baked Yank lady had sneered once. It was better than
that. We drank tea, Lennis told me a story.*
*A boy had been killed by a bear. Not eaten, just smothered. No
clawmarks. His parents wanted him buried in the churchyard;
the caretakers refused, but the bishop allowed it. So the ash-
es were planted with his neighbours. Lennis had worked as a
lumberman, far back, in '31. They paid him $5 a month. The
whole Opeongo, still lingered then, overgrown lots, and
cabins in ruin, but a few, like the Tubmans, had found work,
though the dream to reach Huron had vanished. As the forest
returned, rich and poor died together. Settlements sparse, or
half-visible. We shook hands and hugged the old couple.*

As we drive back, the valley seems wilder, the road more
steeply inclined. Black-eyed Susans and Michaelmas daisies
grow alongside the paving. The land rolls away to the north,
sunlight glitters on the lakes, half-rotted logs and beams jut
out from the wild woods. The nearest gas station, the local
bait sellers, and a favourite Tim Hortons are not too far away.

FEBRUARY MORNING

Dark windows.
Time blinded by storms
in my skull.
I fall, in slow motion,
but refuse to wake up:
my dreams a faint frost
of unwitting stories,
love winnowed away
by the heart's tired machinery.

Yet grounded in quaint rote
the mind gibbers on.
I stir, and with new breath imagine,
the clear light of spring beneath the snow.

THE VISITOR

I lounge in our cabin at sunset,
meals and then music, the sheltering woods
shroud the hills by the lake.
A blanketed world,
but everything stirring, in hiding.

Between cabin and woodland
the sky growing dimmer,
the air full of shrieks, as if cold piping fear
had engulfed all the small birds.

My wife steps outside.
A moment later she calls.
I push through the doorway,
walk down the driveway, stare past
the tire ruts, the piled-up kindling.
In the thickets of darkness
leaves and bare branches stand out,
changing shape
with my steps or fresh glances.

I speak, but my wife just points upwards.
Small birds flutter round.
On a thick branch
an owl sits unmoving.

The owl gapes, a bolster of barred flesh,
its feathered bulk launched
from the woods down the road.

Its round face with forward-seeking eyes,
dark sockets steady,
keeps watch on the whole scene.

Bird shrieks continue.
We stand there and wait for the kill.

Time passes, the owl moves
at last, rising up,
finds a branch on the gray birch
just beyond our back acres.

From there it stares down.
We wait, staring back.
Long minutes later it vanishes,
its great wings extended,
beating slowly in silence.

The night seems to close in.
We stand without words,
then retreat to the cabin,
thinking of powers in the darkness,
both ancient and beautiful,
and small birds in panic,
like us, taking flight,
when the eyes of the hunter
release them.

II STAGES

BETWEEN THE ACTS

At half past one she floated lightly
across the telephone,
shock waves rebounded
from her shaped voice,
the silence took on
a poignant boredom.

When they met at last
her reputation had shaken
the voices of men
describing her past,
none of whom had known her
in the sharpest sense.

Even so, there was time enough
for him to imagine
every stone she might turn
in his life—and what she buried
just then in the flesh of his mind
kept him counting
the hours between meetings,
the minutes between the hours.

This story has no ending.
there is nothing to report
of sad conclusions, happy issues,
the meetings go on
toward nothing inevitable,

though he paces up and down
and her hand falters slightly
when she knocks on the door.

A LITTLE TOWN ON THE RIDEAU

In this small town
a cloudy spring day,
rain falling softly
on quiet streets and houses,
or neighbours' green backyards.

Brick storeys, silent bedrooms,
old attics full of shadows,
all nearly invisible,
while log houses stand out
with bright chinking,
near limestone walls of cottages,
darkened by rain.

We stroll past unplanted gardens,
the play structures empty,
sheds with sagging doors, bare maples,
a thicket of branches,
porches and chimneys,
a quiet world, scrub fields
that stretch to the woods
beyond some tin roofs
and the old weathered church spire.

Soon we pause for a moment
by the swing bridge, the river.
My wife takes my hand,
the roar of the water attracts us,

a new kind of silence arises
inside our lost selves
still edged by the last ice.

BLITHE SPIRITS AND COWARDLY PLAYWRIGHTS

The playwright summons humour to laugh at loss,
well-heeled souls in the drawing room so icily vacant.
A "medium" programmed to ravish good taste and décor
ends up on her back, and quite clearly a bore.
Ah yes, better cute fellows than all these male-female
fakers. Cold hell between husband and wives
neither memory nor action, nor wit that can summon
essentials. Neat clothing, sly glances, clipped ardour
must preside over contact. The middle class blessings
dressed up, lacking content, and quite soon demolished.
Nothing lives beneath gestures or sly tones!
"I'm clever," the playwright decides,
"I'll show you your real selves,
I've created a world that's no better than you are.
You'll laugh at my stale wit, my bad jokes,
Just out of stupidity, heading for death
like the rest of us, bloodless and silly.
When's the next showing? You think you'll survive
to enjoy it? I hope so, since profit's at least quite consoling."

THE STAGES OF LOVE

While shadows stole the room we waited,
Afraid to push our feelings far.
Our loyalties, our fears—all stated,
While shadows stole the room we waited.
Deep passions stirred, we hesitated,
The cold moon rose, and one bleak star.
While shadows stole the room we waited
Afraid to push our feelings far.

Love stunned us but we found a way
To hold those other lives together.
Plain marriage, children, day by day,
Love stunned us but we found a way.
Let no one doubt us, no one say
Fidelity was not our weather.
Love stunned us but we found a way
To hold those other lives together.

We meet as strangers under fire
As if recoiling from the past.
Does guilt or merely art require
We meet as strangers under fire?
Such brave safe conducts of desire
Are not what we had hoped would last.
We meet as strangers under fire
As if recoiling from the past.

THAT AFFAIR

We climbed up the mural to meet,
dizzy with uncivil love.
The office grew conditioned
to our shocking hours,
took final notice
of its own shortcomings.
Thrown inside all gaps and angles
we gave up everything to cry
not there, not there
at the spotlights—
found doorways, stairs,
and disembodied heads,
walls blank as cheese.
With minds rolled backward by stages
we could play every scene
of the uncertain future—
orchards on bedrock,
such gambits.
People were bound to conceal,
their particular horror
of our bootlegged love—
and when it was over their relief
like a storm that would never break,
darkened every streetcorner.

POEMS FOR A JAPANESE SILK SCREEN

The beach endures the fury of the waves.
Under my gaze the bare-breasted woman sleeps.

The moonlight finds its way
from her eyes to mine.

Spring,
the melting snow
her smile.

Tiny bare feet on hard stone.
The river rushes by,
Oh, the sweetness of flesh!

Her white body,
a terrifying arch
in the darkness.

Her fingers caress her new lover.
They make love without thinking of me,
filling up my room with emptiness.

BLUES

Look out for the easy.
He's a dancing killer.
He swallows women
like sarsaparilla.
For what's in his pocket,
the sun and the moon
they rock him into heaven
with a fancy tune.

They'll do for his sorrow
when no bird's in hand,
whistle his troubles
to the promised land.

Some women dance the piper
and others pay.
It's a shame to sleep alone
on a rainy day.

And women and dogs
they get kicked around.
He'll be gone in the morning
and he won't make a sound.

Lady, smooth your pillows
for another guest.
No man ever
lays his mind to rest.

SNOWQUEEN SUTRA

The snowqueen wields recipes, mantras.
Her rites are forgotten, her spells incoherent,
Yet she's always beside you, white teeth sharpened from
childhood.

She peels in the dark, to offer her praise to stalactites.
Shopping for bargains on Thursday,
writing lists in lipstick on her kneecaps,
the snowqueen is your first teacher, the flower of kindergarten,
Mom and the heroes, your maiden aunt, moondust, a song.

She is the delicate tracery on the windows of winter.
The black hole in your quantum of space,
an insidious torment.
The snowqueen's changing fire to sadness,
forcing truth to a web, she widows light.

You'll meet her on your last flight to Paris;
she always goes stand-by.
Corner her and she'll disappear, preferring older men
on whom the smell of death is fresh.

Marry the snowqueen, she'll dress you
in halter and false breasts.
At precious moments, when desire fails,
she's alive in the shadows.
Her mirror cracks in your hands, she discovers deception.
A splinter enters your eye, you surrender your heart.

THE WAGER

We gambled,
not to be shaken down
by the earth.
Lucky,
I kiss the clean skull
behind your face.

SONIA

Fullrigged Sonia comes flying from the far corners.
Her cordage coils to threaten
calm space at dead centre
down in the deep hold
where tar smells, sweat smells mingle,
and love is a perishable cargo.

A freelance dapper traveller
she stretches dreams into history,
hitch-hiking with the legions,
rolling over the Appenines,
curling up in old trenches and foxholes
dancing for sailors—
as they speak her name softly
her body bursts like a star on their tongues.

Sonia loves women
yet consorts with our maimed world
in half-sleazy bars.
Businessmen sanction and pay for her sorrow.
She bikes every day through the labyrinth,
is questioned once too often at the border,
makes love in six languages,
in the fifty positions,
sleeps nude while the sea laps softly at her body—
bronzed men walk away reacquainted with the bliss of dawn.

On the great and impossible circuit
between life and desire
too many falter,
while she remains faithful
to the small arcana of her own impostures—
but don't touch her, my friend,
during high tide and moonlight
she'll make you cry as from a nightmare
in the arms of some lost perfect woman.

SONG FROM THE NEW MEXICO COMMUNE, 1974

Oh, the dark gods are waiting
way down where your mind
lapses out into silence
& your senses go blind.
In the marrow of night
life is born in a spark
and the dark gods are burning
alive in the dark

You think about love
and start up a cage.
You let yourself in
beat the bars in your rage.
Don't think about love
don't make chains of your tongue.
The dark gods are waiting
till your logic is done.

When you go to a woman
don't follow your will.
Follow your body
till your body rides still.
Climb into the darkness,
let love be your touch,
When two bodies go lightly
no love is too much.

But don't talk of sorrow
don't measure your blood
you'll wake up forever
if you drown in the flood.
The stars are your fellows,
the flowers are your kind,
and your body's a god
that will swallow your mind.

LUMINA II

A fool to handshake fame
ignoring wise old teachers,
espousing hell's sweet routes.

*

eyes, hair, quiet smiles,
love's irrational preference
for a singular thing.

*

He lived in the past
Where the rent was low.

*

doped limbs
stretched for dollars.
street girl dancing.

*

young lovers kiss,
a foolish thought
blooms in my head.

*

not-haves resent
what the haves have:
Nothing.

     *

At cultivating colleagues
a master ...
if art were recommendation.

     *

researchers gloat
over flaws in the famous
whose lives they pen and pan.

     *

old trees cut down,
invisible shadows
on the overpriced lots.

     *

at the Delphi ruins
a tourist bus,
waiting for the gods.

THE SPINNING WHEEL

Meine Ruh ist hin,
Mein Herz ist schwer;
Ich finde sie nimmer
Und nimmermehr.
  (Johann Wolfgang von Goethe)

She ditches her sorrow.
Domes flash in sunlight,
Spires point a magical blue.
The wheel turns, such a face!
Two eyes, a mouth, and two hands weaving stories.
Words may dissemble, but never the art
at her fingertips. Clear strength
of mind moves the world,
captures the stranger gone begging
from dim house to house in the village.
At her door the poor fellow peels off
his threadbare coat, asks for supper.
"I cook as I conjure," she warns him.
Then opens the cupboard, revealing
gingerbread hearts, wine in crystal,
As she sings, he discovers
the joy of wild things
in the borderless night.

Soon the village dissolves.
The man disappears
in the quiet of the forest.

Before morning
she dares to untangle
flowers from her rare fire—
in a mirror, a prison, a garden,
a circle of stars will appear.

ROOMMATES

Lost themselves three years running
in the same direction,
     dark girl and blonde,
wore the skin of their attics like minks—
shared mum mirrors of pot and Picasso,
two-in-the-morning music of high times.
Petted to sleep like the great women
     of history, munching chocolates.
Dark girl, treated for early mustache, hysteria,
slipping naked into a raincoat, off for church,
the blonde loving to melt exquisitely
     into the eyes
of every man who felt rainbows at the end
     of her shudder.
And sometimes letters from the mothers,
                    catatonic,
beaten by their men, perfumed wisdom—
You can always come home for the weekend
though the daddy in the shadow,
     the emasculate
Santa Claus under an elm tree by heaven
strums his guitar, and is waiting—
     bus schedules,
lists of psychiatrists, blackbook of lovers
     in his pocket,
the big hole in his mind stuffed
     with gingerbread—
everything a girl needs to marry a brute

and hide under a pillow,
just a question of transferring effects
    from the suburbs.
Girls, it's a good pad, and—pull up
    your pants—
the best cave's Platonic.

TO THE GOOD WIFE

Your love, your blindspot, blurs from day to day
the visions it grew up to see.
Springs die to a trickle while you ride the river.
Branches pricked with buds you snap tartly,
Every day down thin back alleys, heave your hope,
like a fat wife pitching laundry on the line.
Everything's a nuisance, in your charity
patience a last resource.
Always alert for the unforgivable
you're not immune to the disease
of being single-minded,
a jingo who tears lampshades out of her skin
to prove the empire of her loving heart.

If homesickness is the most I can plead
I'll bring my case close to home,
a tired colonist who detests the climate
but returns again and again,
out of a sentiment blunter than passion
and sharper than custom, to your sullen port.

STRICT VOYEUR LOVE SONG

My wife finds her way to another lover.
The spring is full of innuendos.
She is taken by his eyes, face, body.
He is taken by her eyes, face, body.
They admire each other constantly in secret.
Lunch on the grass may be preface to nothing.
She thinks a lot about his strange tattoos.
He is asking her to go to bed.
Stopping to buy wine and condoms,
She feels fear and joy.
In the motel they fall shyly together.
Touching hair, thighs, stroking, kissing.
Dumfounded quickly between the sheets
the secret animals aroused take over.
When he enters between her legs she remembers
love's sharp blur of insinuation.
Resting inside circles of arms,
shower games naked kiss some splashing.
TV bawls away in the background.
They don't feel like finishing the wine.
Outside the city is otherwise busy.
Driving back they begin to notice it's late.
Meet again warily wanting more and less.
With many etceteras, a few surprises,
he phones her by day to continue between them.
One night she walks in her sleep toward his name.
No reason there for discretion's silence.
Though inmates may reckon a bedroom's terror,

what can the body betray but its wonder?
The brave thigh hath a life of its own
says the small bird of imagination.

A LITTLE TEETH-GNASHING IN MEMORY
OF YOUR INNER OGDEN

Hello, old friend, I have this to say:
the world you live in day by day
continues every morning with little change,
same old intensity and range:
sunlight and snow or grass and clouds and light.
You wake up stiff and groaning,
newborn, but quite fresh, after another night.
Your body almost tuned to face the world.
Your safe enclosures—house and rooms and bed still here—
pedestrians tramping or driving quickly by
to earn their predictable livings, and few wonder why
the sameness of their routines stays secure.
No wars nearby, no sudden revolution,
a bit more discontent, and new pollution.
While everything you take for granted, is given,
your body strong, your mind alert, unshriven
thoughts and dreams, seem well-preserved.
Although your wilder longings are not served,
those naked beauties, distant pictures, conjured up
by money would be easily detected
by therapists trained to probe your heart,
infected images to keep you on the mark,
so that you never doubt that life is stark
for those without access to agile flesh, a breed
unlike a good wife, to fill your instant need,
ignoring their own demands while you succeed
in bed or on the floor to come apart
and prove that lust is central to your heart.

It's never quite a day like that, my friend.
It seems your visions have nearly reached the end
of pleasure to become the weakest part
of life that's never cool or smart
without new lineaments of desire,
 or sweet things that human need will hire
to keep the peace in times of bitter stress.
It's just another day, I guess,
sad, but quite soon experience will show
just how far your puny drives will go
to wed you to the human race
in its sly postures of disgrace.
To make quite certain you forget
how luckily your life is set
for love's creation, and I'll bet
you rate the best too low forever.
So I'll remind you to dissever
wish from reality of bone.
How failure came, left you alone,
your head bashed down on
blocks of stone,
your mind a blank, your strength
no longer part of your stopped, shaken heart.
It was your wife who saved your skin.
She made that healing bunch take you in.
She waited and watched and counted the days,
and kept herself focused and remained pretty sure
she could lead you back to a world you'd endure,
this world, where you wake up to slow, perfect days
in which you remain sensible and sane,

despite your ever-present quite inane
wish for romances unsuitable to age,
where you sit in your office groping for life,
not remembering that dark figure of the recent year,
one who will, I`m afraid, once again suddenly appear
and greet you with his or her impersonal sinister laugh,
heard but hardly welcomed by every human heart since
the dawn.
Yes, thinking persons, even you, must die, although life may
go on.
So sit up straight and greet the lingering world, my old friend.
Expect the shadow and prepare for the end.
Your quest for routine joy has a terminal date.
Reach out, don`t complain and be strong.
Believe in that secret melody you carry along,
sometimes lost, and yet pulsing forever
in your life`s inexplicable and complex song.

COCKTAILS IN ROME

We meet to drown a quarrel
    and concoct one, my Catholic hostess and I,
        stirring dogma with cinzano,
            her infallible repartees
                defying all my gracious trimming toasts.

Having sampled, from politeness,
    the hors d'oeuvres of her richer truth,
        I refrain unorthodoxly from her main
            invitation to self-indulgence.
                (Say my digestion is weak).

At last she names my abstinence
    heretical, her ultramontane thundering
        wit scatters our truce
            like Moses' rock old confidence
                of eye for eye.
                (Her eye burkes my damnation but not my judgment).

Then, white gloves flapping out,
    dove-winged, she mounts the inspiration
        of her anger, abjures before her friend,
            the cardinal, the day's list that brought me.

"Invitations in good faith accepted
    make vespers truer than capitulation,"
        I protest from a corner,
            proud of my dry biscuit and water.
                remembering Canossa.

A TRUE STORY

I wrote a four-hundred page novel so as to be a voyeur
at the love feast of a tall, slender girl
and an older woman, a blonde witch, who enchants her.
Life imitates art, but not exactly.
My imagination is still the room that contains them,
and allows them to grapple; but I have become my
own character:
a white bear raging and tearing at the ice around their bed.

JUMPING OFF

I can't help it.
It's like a ship I'm sick of.
The mast is wobbly, deck warped by too many high seas—
a train that's careening on tired rails,
a car that's getting hard to start,
a wagon mired in mud.

This has been going on for a long time.
The passengers don't need me.
Bailing out isn't painful.
It's a whole new experience,
walking with another body
through transparent earth
into time
without motion.

This is the thing you do
at the end of the journey.

Wave at the world
and get free.

SNAPSHOT

81

A shutter opens on the light.
We conspire with the sun.
Love moves through time,
endless space.
Yet fixed in this place
she and I almost one.

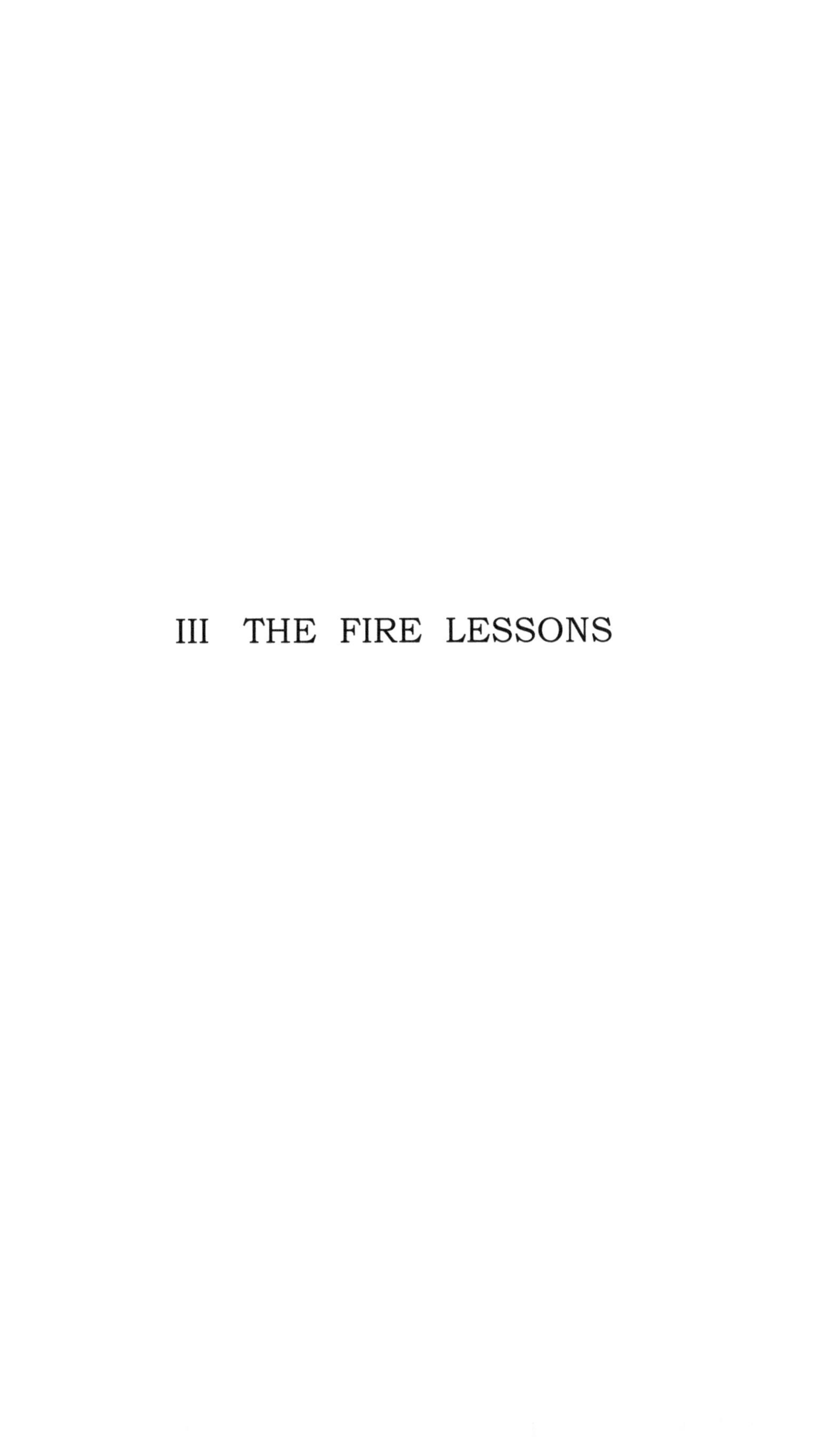

III THE FIRE LESSONS

BUDDHA IN THE BASEMENT

The Buddha floats out of the basement.
It's spring in our back yard.
I open the shed and look round.
The world is still buying and selling.
New wars are predicted, continue,
old spades and hoes put to use,
though they can't dig out greed,
or touch the root violence.
Soil and seed are no better,
yet they flower every spring.
Things of the world seem askew.
Bag the leftover leaves, tend the pond,
cut up firewood, set down the Buddha
 in the heart of the garden.
A good time of year,
but despite our best efforts
and what grows in the home soil—
children and vegetables
the joy of the house—
the season holds back.
I live even now with the bare trees,
lost in desire for what's vanished.
Wooed by a wise text and teachers,
I pick up the Buddha,
brush off the dust and the winter,
long for the cold stone to speak
to rehearse our sad journeys of souls,
to lift us beyond the half-human.

Yet I know, despite hope, a new season,
that the spirit is locked in the body,
and even Siddhartha's rare vision
will dissolve in ephemeral light.

CONFRONTATIONS

All makeup, tight clothes and anger
the tall mother shoves and slaps
her son, who doesn't cry. She hardly
stops screaming. She's shopping
after all, so no one intervenes.
The little boy, frozen, stares past her.
 Perhaps he sees the future.

On the busy thoroughfare
the Fat Boy is beating up the Thin.
Violent punches to the head and down he goes,
crawling away, bleeding. People walk past in silence
and do nothing. The violence continues.
Freedom of expression.

THE FIRE LESSON

The fire roars.
Seven children wake
in their rooms upstairs.
They can't escape the flames.
They are screaming now
like their mother.
She jumps through a window.
Later, in the hospital they tell her
what she cannot believe.
We read this in the papers.
Everyone is sick inside.
It's as if a great hand
reached down
to wipe out
her whole life and happiness.

No one understands.
And if anyone asked,
not even God could give a reason
why we should believe in anything
but pain and accident and death.

These fall on us out of the blue
from heavens of source-fire and darkness,
from close, distant spaces
where God remains absent forever.

NIGHT VIGIL

Your pity proves hellish, remorseless.
Two women, eaten alive, keep on singing.
Technology serves them. Clever inventors
created a new world to rise up and save us.
Image and word, even art, in the codes of the present.
Life broken down and then processed.
Wires share the icons of living. We find
what we need when our own moments,
tragic or locked in, are quite blank.

Something in me,
in bed dim and tired,
called for song.
Hadn't I heard Auger herself in Handel
deliver fierce beauty? In a minute my screen
found her and I knew what I wanted.
Just *Morgen*, it seemed best, just *Morgen*.
We all need a new morning,
especially at night in a friendless room.
Her dawn was full of sunset's loving darkness, a
Strauss dream translated by her sweet voice and time.
It was almost more than I could bear when I thought of her
late life, and I begged the machine for a new birth.

There was the other, the fast blonde,
no longer flirting with love. Once Solti
got her on stage in Chicago, how sedate,
reassuring. *Spring, September, In the Evening,*

above all that sleep in which the winged soul hovers.
The violin, the horns, and she almost broke down
until, lifted by a grateful audience, she smiled and bowed.
Not thinking of the tumours that would come.

After this, with two women tragically gone,
I begged my machine to release me.
But I needed a third voice, something strong,
dark nature found and resisted, but not forever.
My player gave me Sibelius, the seventh and final;
the clock moved. It was late, past one, and Bernstein
raised his arms, Bernstein danced, in the wells
of this brief, endless music, with its solemn grandeur
never false, only deeply consoling. A revelation faded into night.

I flipped off our human invention, the ingenious construction.
That other world vanished, the wonders of art
and commitment.
I was left with myself, the self-removed, an uncertain body.
At the window I could see the burning distant sky,
its images ordered by strong vanished minds,
its numbers recounted by new thoughts, full of
wonder. I continued to reach out, to treasure,
to share hope. I listened for earth's songs,
human faces and bodies, my machinery silent,
my night vigil transformning dreams.

DNA—A CLERIHEW

Watson and Crick
performed a neat trick
they got the world keen
on exploiting the gene.
They showed how a suture
could sew up our future,
and made "Mother Nature"
extinct nomenclature.

UNDERGROUND STORY

The man still tells a story of a boy,
who rode the subway with his father once.
A safe weekend rush up Lexington, the subway
with its dirt-smeared windows, near empty,
taking the curves, wheels roaring,
it swung by lighted walls in the labyrinth,
grinding from one blank stop to the next.
Yet at home things had improved, his mother,
safe from an illness, his sisters ensconced with their
aunts, the kid's mind full of good stories, comics,
cheap bound classics, though the war still reflected
its terrors, far magic spheres flashing uncles and
battles, and fast Sherman tanks just destroyed, the
family would move from one flat to another, stirring up
violent new street boys, their power-shouts and
gestures, but he had the good books and comics to live
with, piled up in his bedroom. And this day,
his dad, without growling or swearing, pointed a seat,
kept his critical mouth shut. The boy remembered
then, as if from some lost world of story, the tales
of his comic book heroes. His dimpled Cagney smile
like a shield protected his shyness. He began to unfold
a fine tale, one kept in mind from his last read, recited as
the train thundered on.

Who remembers what characters lived again? Superman,
Batman, the Flash, the Star-Spangled Kid, Captain Marvel?
The train seemed to fill with their costumes, their wild flights

and struggles. Every plot twist, each struggle between hero and villain, sprang from his sentences, and soon caught his father's attention. The older man stared, gaped, and waited, even a stranger looked up. The boy's story continued, full of improvised changes, plot shifts, bold characters. When he'd finished, he sat up quite proudly, with a broad smile. The stranger stared at his father. "That boy sure can tell a story."

Then the train stopped. Father and son wandered out, speechless, pushing through bare littered tunnels, past billboards, locked exits. They came on a shabby newsstand; the old seller glanced from the shadows. His newspapers screamed of new battles. The boy suddenly remembered a Greek myth and another old man, Charon, who steers the dead across the deep river of death. Bodies took off now from fields and foxholes, flew into the grim boat. That was a great story. But of course he'd get out of this subway, though else-where the killing continued. "That guy back there was right," his father said, less resistant than usual, for once almost pleased. "That was some talk you did, with your reading. All those heroes, adventures. But they won't get you a nickel when you need it." They pushed through the gates, climbed back to the canyons of the streets. The skyscraper windows flashed sunlight. High up, men worked, leaning over from their airy platforms. *"Charon will never touch them,"* the boy told himself. "Don't start that again," his father said. "I heard enough for one day. You and your pipe-dreams. You'll be lucky if you end up washing windows on a building! Comic books won't do you no good when you have to earn a living. I could tell you a few things about life…but forget it. We'll go home and eat now." The kid listened, nodded, not looking

at his father, keeping silent as the city roared around them,
while beneath them, the underground, alive with its dreams
and its hungers, still waited for new stories.

PRIMEVAL LANDSCAPE (TRANSLATION OF "URLANDSCHAFT" BY STEFAN GEORGE)

From gloomy pines
an eagle soars on high.
A wolf-pair prowl the glade,
drink at the stream,
stand guard beside their young.

Down needled paths
shy deer come, drink, and flee.
One victim never leaves the marsh
and dies beyond the darkness of the wood.

Not far away
the overgrown thicket hides
deep roots and traces of a strength
infecting fields. The white sun's
blade of light confirms the reek of earth

where primal sires and dams
have toiled, and sown a fate
for races still to come.

THE DEVELOPERS

*(I struggle to explain, as the ghost of Percy Shelley, poet of
anger and human perfection, stands by, with much better
words, in a far distant sphere)*

In this town they tear down fine old places.
The bulldozers come, the men with new plans,
the lovers of profit, the shapers of false dreams,
minds to make changes, "improvements,"
to upturn rough freedom, destroy old designs.
They sell their smooth worlds in power pamphlets.

Rough fields, long neglected, slum housing,
old factories—most people ignore them,
except for the visionaries, the good politicians,
the preachers of humane creation,
who understand failure and loss
and work to transform them,
while developers, the city's cruel saviours,
build profit.

And what have they done for the future?
Before their transgressions, a freshness,
a grand emancipation of display;
a running amuck of wrinkled branches, a twist of thorns,
flowers springing up among just balancing rocks—
the revelings of an almost ancient ease—
once life remained ripe to improve our potential.

Once, sunlight patterned itself on receptive grass,
and gave an emblazoned torpor to the afternoons;
the stir-enshrouded thickets had their secrets,
and all the sudden accidental places
of nature were full of song.
Then came the developers: soon lost was the wisdom
of old, well-loved places, the foolish gardens,
echoes of Eden, all exchanged for the wonders of money.

Developers! Polished floors; money's steps unrelenting;
The calm commingling of stockbroker and politician,
hired labour; machines made to order, and those houses,
staged rooms fed with false scripts, new homes for the half-
rich, prosperity in chrome and black, humanity in motion.
Backwards.

Each fool's fetish dance brings success
to the bankers, investors with inhuman skills,
the high rollers most likely soon sold out
as their conjured-up palaces vanish.
Later on saved by malingering issues,
unfazed by the lessons of greed, the developers
serve their own profits, as democracy fails.

We await the neglected devisers,
shapers of wild risk and dream,
bold thinkers, who long for the future
and put forth astonishing life charts.
It's time to discount the false prophets,
to cast off their profiting half-life.
To find rich new visions and live them
in worlds where our debt is our freedom.

HARVEST SUPPER

Everybody quiet. It's time to clean out the ghosts
with the same spells that invoked them.
Uncork the dry red, slash leaves from that tangle
hiding the big stones. Pay no mind to old writing
scratched under moss. Seize the wild vine,
to be draped around the girl who looks best
in least. Take the corn ears and roast them
and let fly with butter and salt, and no lewd jokes
when there's time for right action tomorrow.

This is an honest-to-god holiday, put down the chainsaw,
climb off the tractor, rest your butt on the earth.
Let the cows graze ribboned with light near the house.
Let everything happen, nobody forcing the issue.
There's the fire, clean burning, so toss in the rubbish,
old newspapers full of war PR profit,
(but save the obits, which make good reading in retirement)
Save the reviews discreetly for the back house;
toss in the mortgage, we're moving out pronto,
heading off to the boondocks where the spirit so lightly
slips anchor.

Fuel the fire higher with debts and compulsions,
loud static to foul up the peace of the day,
when nothing's enough you caress breast and bottle,
your head wallows, your hands are more than idle.
Burn every injunction, all platitudes gratis
from MPs in hock to the language, then stand back

to avoid inhaling the stink of your virtue.
Look, it's OK, your liver can live with the strain.
The omens are right for a booze-up,
turn handsprings or stagger erect to the bushes.
If the lady can stand you, she's worth all the trouble.
You'll make it, for once, without silly palaver.
With sharp eyes find shapes in the clearings,
A long-haired ex-hippie with small cloven feet
who makes a racket when he's stoned, which is always.
He gave up his guitar long ago for a flute,
patron of the first comers, the early risers,
who settled down in happy places
and said fuck the snow, there's fire in our guts—
they blessed the uncertain springs, the darkest water.

Watch out for the messenger,
wise guy with a pickup, the old crook,
rides over to tell you the good news,
you won the lottery—and there's only one small catch!

Or him with the green thumb, the home brew,
who covers your house with prismatic vines.
When the door jams—in case of fire—go back to the orgy
he's conjured in the rec room you never built.

Then meet the lady champion, dead-shot with the bright bow,
you blink only once at her beauty.
Her aim has nothing to do with your
target, her heels shade you in the sunlight, dazzled.

Drive out such powers at your peril,
alive in the woods, in the deep caves
numisma of lost light, the founders,
who gift us with skills we've remembered:
how to build walls and roof, to plant trees,
to set grain and vine—an almost common knowledge,
though unpracticed—but to winch out of dreams
the music of figures, to let body flail
in images veined to the fingertips,
to lie slack in sunlight and occupy
indolence—too much trouble by far!

Everybody quiet. One more thought for the stones.
They make a cairn over history,
its losses mulled and half-reckoned
by hunters and farmers who imagined
so many wild things, but not change.

And welcome the gods of the harvest
with tipped glass and firm mind
may they slip lightly into existence,
claiming lost trails of signs
faint as moonlight half-buried
in black mud:
How naked our lives wear,
bodiless in bedlam,
until we lose our mortal skins.

THE OUTSIDERS: TWO SPECIES

1) *The Manatee*

I've lately met the manatee,
who calmly browses by the sea,
avoiding sun and salt and speed,
he lives to linger and to feed.
No leaping dolphin, he abhors
the busy life that rings his shores—
a vegan with no need to kill
he dozes and then eats his fill.
His sombre gray and Zeppelin shape
will cause no tourist's eyes to gape.
Mere humans yawn and turn away
while he goes trawling through the day.
He drifts and dreams and surely dotes
on everything but motorboats,
a mammal who knows Zen by nature
and not by foreign nomenclature.
Beyond his world we humans play,
we carve and calculate and stray.
We boast and try to make our mark
and fight off visions of the dark,
but in a dream this dwindling race
of blimps with paddle-tails, finds grace.
While we build castles on the sand,
they float, a slow enduring band,
and know the seas wear out the land.

2) *The Sasquatch*

The Sasquatch, sighted now and then,
avoids the crooked paths of men—
and women too (I swear I meant)—
for Darwin's Origin and Descent
suggest he tolerate no rival
whose habits threaten his survival.
And yet his mere existence turns
on evidence that science spurns:
he suffers through uneasy dreams
and is more nervous than he seems
to anxious hunters, eager questers
and varied status quo molesters.

The Sasquatch daily on the run
cavorts beneath the midnight sun;
A thing of fancy, beast of air,
he revels in not being there,
And life of quasar, as of quark.
shows absence too can make its mark.
He rises up in monstrous shape
but will predictably escape
the reach of sense, the range of reason,
though moonshine offers open season.

So every night, to test his worth
the Sasquatch bellows, pointing north:
a sleep beneath the northern sky
can give reality the lie.

It washes out concrete objections
declared too soon in earth's convections.

Pure science, rarely lost from sight
stands up and roars with all its might
(though sometimes doubts creep in at night).
Auroras burn across the sky,
the Sasquatch answers with a cry.
The woods are old, the tundra stark,
and while the polar foxes bark
a wild dream wakens in the dark.

ON A SCIENCE FICTION WRITER

You crouched over yesterday's paper,
cursed out your car.
In love like the rest with the anodyne habits
of a slipshod culture—
when over your left shoulder they flung the first light,
someone sharing its eerie dimensions
with the tramping horses of your dreams—
a fugue of memories new
in the machinery of just now,
every contour perfectly resplendent
as Albireo doubled on a calm night,
bold in his gold-blue youth.

So the earth changed expression—
a child remembering its birthday,
the tired cities lost their tainted skins,
whales signalled from the clear ocean depths,
the powerhouse of the blood phased in
a love of common hardware,
and you remembered, not for the last time,
how lonely we have always been.

POE'S GYROSCOPE

*"The rays of the moon seemed to search the very bottom
of the profound gulf; but still I could make out nothing
distinctly, on account of a thick mist in which everything
there was enveloped, and over which there hung a mag-
nificent rainbow, like that narrow and tottering bridge
which Mussulmen say is the only pathway between Time
and Eternity."*

(A Descent into the Maelström).

Spin gyroscope
across a string
and watch it shape
the bave descant
of silver wing
by careful hand
held straight in air.
And hear the spin
of arcs in time
and feel the taut
true thrill of point,
the balanced wave
of metal sphere—
but time curves in
and arcs cut wide
on finite strings,
their crazy spin
of power runs down,
a dizzy sweep

invades the air,
and as the swing
of metal slows
the silver cell
the moving rings
give up to silence
hectic songs
until decline
wipes out the whir
of sphere on string,
and all the sweep
of silver wing
can never fix
the music here
nor can string find
the perfect sphere,
though tightly held
by fingers' skill.
The fading song
the wobbling light
the sinking circle
arc in air,
make all of motion's
round despair
go on, go on,
and down through air
that metal dance
must fall at last
from spin and drone
must fall through time
and space
like stone.

LUMINA III

Great Poseidon
holding his nose
swims past the oil rig.

*

Large and beautiful
bright red
tasteless tomatoes.

*

A shrine full of tourists.
mystery fizzles
like a stale Coke.

*

Violent protests,
factions ravage
subliminal virtues.

*

Meticulous as always
he cut his throat
with Occam`s razor.

*

in the narrow street
the child shrieks,
a car`s terror

                *

Spirit, the ergot
of love's
sweetest visions.

                *

Every day we just talk,
he never mentions
exploring your body.

                *

Easy to forget
the most important dreams.

DISCOVERY

The machines, suburban stores, art galleries,
the tallest buildings, the greatest bridges
having vanished at the first attack
not much was left for future investigation,
and when, a thousand years later,
following several dark ages and despoilations,
alien visitors finally had a look
at the ruins of our twenty-first century world,
there was little to indicate high civilization.
Few tools had survived, fewer hints of old lifestyles.
The collages, shopped photos, bare porno downloads,
known to have existed were not found,
but cyber space coughed up its dissonant memories
in blips flashing greed and mere passionate echoes,
a world of desire and of corpulent selfhood,
locked once and forever in the dim Oz of time.

HOMECOMING

The planets multiply, all empty—
as we knew before we came.
How frightening the probes
that revealed, all those centuries,
such endless blank faces of snow,
empty sockets of craters, the ridged teeth
of mountains, planets like stone skulls;
or fat gas maremmas, where thought never coiled up,
no green sprig of joy springing anywhere
in those blind, bitter wastes.
Was it worth voyaging then,
on a thin thread of time,
all the light years between
expectation and certainty
extinguished on landing,
as if being there were the exile
of thought from its object?
Many times doubt rose like a storm
of derision, our skills mocking hope
as we hove to and gazed, stopped to measure.
Many times, lifting off, we despaired at the blank trail
leading nowhere from somewhere.
But later, grown old, weary searching,
we followed rare truths like faint suns,
back across well-charted spaces,
counting the way stations,
numbering, naming, the wanderers
knew each from the others:

Erebus, Doom and the Dark Land,
Titan and Cauldron, Hell's Rim and Deep,
strong links of an iron chain
that we climbed up to cast off,
a stark dream like a riddle
recalled out of sleep with no answer . . .
Circling homeward at last,
bound from darkness to darkness,
we discovered, as if for the first time,
our own precious alien earth.

CLARK KENT IN OLD AGE

Weightless, inside this mortal suit,
the tonnage of years on a stick,
l clutch at each clue to the old life.
An orphan of suffering, in search of
miraculous time, lovely muscle
of wish become flesh, but the changes!
One arm and a stiffly drawn head
twisted upward, l stumble . . .
They help me as much as they can,
their regret green as once their envy
grew, green as Krypton—a slow rot
begins in the brain, in the crotch,
superlatives die before the rest.
Only comic? Never mind if the elegy's
coined for your cat, or your goldfish—
you imagined it all, Lear too, and
Samson. Jobbers and sad old men
as well as princes of royal blood
hire fools or are aped
by their lackeys. Die, decline,
fade away or are forgotten.
Hero and clown all at once,
Unreal but never spurious,
l carried what I could
of your first lust for story.
Consider at least your own joy,
how the colours moved in your mind
as you dodged through backyards

where not even your X-ray eyes
could see the rubble of your own childhood.
And if you don't pity me
pity at least what your mirror shows
of what you might have been
without fear and the perils
of too much gravity.

MUSIC LESSON

> *He wandered about and finally came to an old tower,*
> *climbed the narrow winding staircase and saw a little*
> *door. There was a rusty key sticking in the lock and when*
> *he turned it, the door sprang open. There, in a little room,*
> *sat an old woman with a spindle, singing, and busying*
> *herself with spinning flax for the future.*
>   *(Variations on a Grimm story for past and future)*

Once a week, the boy was released
to climb like Dornröschen
up the old winding stairs
to a small room
where the air smelled of death,
chairs and floorboards creaked
and the crucifix
gleamed like a dagger
in the half-dark.

The swish of gowns
made a medieval sound,
like a slow spool of sorrows
unwinding dire occasions,
while the ghosts of dead heroes
countersunk long ago
in the coffins of hopeful America,
fled their last refuge
in our adolescent hearts.
The world closed in

on our innocence,
our fears denounced us
without naming names.
The boy sat shamefully
among the converted
and wished himself a Jew,
or Prince Charming.
Wheels spun in his head
his faith taxed hard by the loopholes
of virtue, by the energy
bursting his gown,
when a bald, queer man
dashing as Rumplestiltskin,
appeared with a message.

"On this earth
so much that is destructive
and so little that is creative,"
quoted the teacher,
whose world embraced Mozart,
Strauss and Mahler,
Stravinsky, Ives and Barber,
great halls, and maestros
with magic hands.

In a new kind of ghetto
the boy heard his summons,
his body shook on its anchor,
freed from the grammar
of circumstance,

consumed by a cold blue flame—
art's inscrutable auspices.

Decades unrolled
without harmony:
the weary jungle soldiers,
the new plagues,
and mad politicians
who bombed the "insane"
in Grenada.
Iraq, Rwanda,
Kabul and Gaza,
torn children lost
in the lifeless dark—
cacophonies of history.

Now the old man climbs the stairs,
dazed by his own indignation
drifts from one sleep to another.
At the shut room's threshold,
life seizes his heart
with the rectitude and anger
of a crone.

Over him, over kingdoms
of closure
the sour note of memory
hangs like a curse.

Yet startled quite suddenly
into childhood, he endures each betrayal,
while music, its measured skill strong
through the soul's trial, releases,
in jubilant sorrow,
the tongues of his mind.
Energy forever, in his own true faithful song,
returns now, along life's weary track
where—magic pleasures sown—
he resists this world's cold silence,
with transformed heart and powers
asserts the consoling voices,
reclaims his own lost hours.

ACKNOWLEDGEMENTS

Most of the poems in The Fire Lessons are new or unpublished. However, a small number have appeared in poetry magazines, e.g., *Poetry Northwest, Salt, The Far Point, Tesseracts*, and *Hierophant*. I have also imported and republished here two previously published poems that seemed compatible with the themes and moods of this collection. I would like to thank a few friends (skilled poets and readers) for helpful suggestions and insights. These include Mark Frutkin, Daniel Boland, Nicola Vulpe, Rosie Dalgliesh, and Marilyn Henighan. Over the years, brief meetings and other personal contacts with writers, some of them famous and notable, have inspired me. Jen Hamilton was once again my gifted designer and patient production manager, and, as always, a pleasure to work with.